The Medieval World

Food and Feasts
in the Middle Ages

Lynne Elliott

Crabtree Publishing Company

www.crabtreebooks.com

Crabtree Publishing Company

www.crabtreebooks.com

PMB 16A, 350 Fifth Avenue
Suite 3308
New York, NY 10118

612 Welland Avenue
St. Catharines
Ontario, Canada
L2M 5V6

73 Lime Walk
Headington
Oxford 0X3 7AD
United Kingdom

Coordinating editor: Ellen Rodger

Project editor: Carrie Gleason

Designer and production coordinator: Rosie Gowsell

Scanning technician: Arlene Arch-Wilson

Pre-press production: Samara Parent

Art director: Rob MacGregor

Project development, editing, photo editing, and layout:
First Folio Resource Group, Inc.: Tom Dart, Jaimie Nathan, Debbie Smith, Anikó Szocs

Photo research: Maria DeCambra

Prepress : Embassy Graphics

Printing: Worzalla Publishing Company

Consultant: Isabelle Cochelin, University of Toronto

Photographs: Alinari/Art Resource, NY: p. 10 (left), p. 16, p. 18 (top right), p. 18 (top left), p. 18 (center right), p. 22, p. 23 (top); Art Archive/Arquivo Nacional da Torre do Tombo Lisbon/Dagli Orti: title page; Art Archive/Biblioteca Estense Modena/Dagli Orti: p. 13 (top), p. 15 (top); Art Archive/Biblioteca Nacional Lisbon/Dagli Orti: p. 10 (right); Art Archive/Bibliothèque Nationale Paris/Harper Collins Publishers: p. 26; Art Archive/Bodleian Library Oxford/Liturg e.36 folio 90v: cover; Art Archive/British Library: p. 29 (top), p. 29 (bottom); Art Archive/Museo Civico Padua/Dagli Orti: p. 27 (top left); Art Archive/Dagli Orti: p. 30 (right); Art Archive/University Library Prague/Dagli Orti: p. 18 (bottom left); Art Archive/Victoria and Albert Museum London/Graham Brandon: p. 21 (bottom); Biblioteca Marciana, Venice, Italy/Giraudon/Bridgeman Art Library: p. 8; Bibliothèque Nationale/Latin 9333 fol 60: p. 11; Bibliothèque Nationale, Paris, France/Giraudon/Bridgeman Art Library: p. 14; Barnabas Bosshart/Corbis/magmaphoto.com: p. 31 (bottom); British Library/Add. 27695 f.14: p. 19 (top); British Library/Add. 42130 f.176: p. 13 (bottom right); British Library/Add. 42130 f.206v: p. 20 (bottom); British Library/Add. 42130 f.207v: p. 20 (top); British Library/Royal 10 E. IV f.58: p. 13 (bottom left); British Museum/Topham-HIP/The Image Works: p. 23 (bottom); John Elk III/Elk Photography: p. 30 (left); Giraudon/Art Resource, NY: p. 27 (bottom right); Mary Evans Picture Library: p. 18 (bottom right); Musée Condé, Chantilly, France/Bridgeman Art Library: p. 7 (top); Musée Condé, Chantilly, France/Giraudon/Bridgeman Art Library: p. 5 (bottom); Nimatallah/Art Resource, NY: p. 17; Gianni Dagli Orti/Corbis/magmaphoto.com: p. 13 (bottom center), p. 31 (top); Phillips, The International Fine Art Auctioneers, UK/Bridgeman Art Library: p. 12; Pierpont Morgan Library/Art Resource, NY: p. 21 (top); Réunion des Musées Nationaux/Art Resource, NY: p. 28

Illustrations: Jeff Crosby: pp. 24–25; Katherine Kantor: flags, title page (border), copyright page (bottom); Margaret Amy Reiach: borders, gold boxes, title page (illuminated letter), copyright page (top), contents page (all), pp. 4-5 (timeline), p. 4 (top), p. 5 (top), p. 6 (all), p. 15 (bottom), p. 19 (bottom), p. 32 (all)

Cover: While nobles dined, they were sometimes entertained by musicians, such as this woman playing a harp.

Title page: People in the Middle Ages drank wine from ewers and flasks and enjoyed different kinds of bread.

Published by
Crabtree Publishing Company

Cataloging-in-Publication Data
Elliott, Lynne.
  Food and feasts in the Middle Ages / Lynne Elliott.
     p. cm. -- (The medieval world)
Includes index.
  ISBN 0-7787-1348-2 (RLB) -- ISBN 0-7787-1380-6 (pbk)
  1. Food habits--History--To 1500. 2. Dinners and dining--History--To 1500. 3. Cookery, Medieval. 4. Civilization, Medieval. I. Title. II. Series.
  Medieval world (Crabtree Publishing Company)
  GT2850.E52 2004
  394.1'2'0902--dc22
                                                     2004000817
                                                     LC

Table of Contents

The Middle Ages

The period in history called the Middle Ages, or the medieval period, began in western Europe around 500 A.D. and lasted until about 1500 A.D. During this time, the most powerful people in society were wealthy nobles, such as kings and great lords, who ruled over large areas of land.

The great nobles gave land, called manors, to less important nobles in return for their advice and their help fighting enemies. Each manor had a castle or manor house where the noble lived and a village with peasants' houses. Some manors also had a church, a mill for grinding grain, and an oven for baking bread. The village was surrounded by fields where crops were grown, meadows where **livestock** grazed, forests with wood for building and cooking, and streams and rivers that provided fish and fresh water.

▶ *In the Middle Ages, the king and great lords held the most power and land, but peasants made up 90 percent of the population and grew almost everyone's food.*

The feudal system develops; rice brought to Spain from the Middle East
700s

European towns and markets grow
900s

Sieves help sift bran from flour to make fine white bread
1066

Fairs bring together merchants from faraway places
1200s

800s
Europeans begin using heavy plows, padded horse collars, and horseshoes

1000s
Water mills used to grind grain into flour

1100s
Increased trade between Europe and the Middle East, India, and Asia

1202
King John of England introduces the first law governing the price of bread

▲ *In medieval times, people around the world grew different kinds of grains. Wheat, barley, and rye were grown in Europe, millet and sorghum were grown in Africa, rice was grown in India and China, and maize, or corn, was grown in North America.*

Working on the Manor

Peasants lived and worked on a manor, renting houses and strips of land from the lord. They paid their rent by working in the lord's fields. They also gave the lord a large portion of the food they grew for themselves and some of the animals they raised.

Peasants produced enough food for everyone on the manor, but during long periods of war, bad crops, or poor weather, there was not enough to eat. In some cases, food shortages led to famines, or widespread starvation.

▶ *Peasants usually worked in the lord's fields two or three days a week, and even more during the busy harvest time.*

European harvests
fail; famine; butter
churn invented
1300

1493–1502
Christopher Columbus
introduces new foods to
Europe after four voyages
to "the New World"

Ideas About Food

For most people in the Middle Ages, the food they ate depended on what they could grow, what was available at local markets, and what they could afford to buy. The diet of the wealthiest people was also influenced by the ideas that medieval doctors and cooks had about food.

People in the Middle Ages ranked everything according to importance, even food. An item's importance was measured by its closeness to heaven. The highest-ranking, or best, foods flew in the sky, close to heaven. These foods included cranes, pheasants, and other birds. The lowest-ranking foods grew in the ground, farthest from heaven. These foods included onions and turnips. The highest-ranking foods were served at nobles' tables, while the lowest-ranking foods were eaten by peasants.

The ideas that wealthy people had about food were also influenced by doctors' opinions. Medieval doctors thought that eating too many raw fruits and vegetables was unhealthy because these foods were "windy," or caused gas and diarrhea. Instead, they advised people to occasionally bake fruit in wine and to cook vegetables in stews. Doctors also advised people to eat bread, which soothed the stomach, and beans, which were nutritious.

▼ From the Sky: Highest ranking

▼ From the Oceans

▼ From the Earth

▼ From Trees and Bushes

▼ From the Ground: Lowest ranking

Cooks' Ideas

By the later Middle Ages, cooks, who prepared food for the wealthy, had developed certain ideas on when foods should be eaten. Light foods, such as melons, cherries, and grapes, were to be served before heavier foods, such as meat, because light foods were easier to **digest** and prepared the stomach for heavier foods. Apples and pears were supposed to be eaten at the end of meals because they prevented other foods from "coming up." Cheese, the heaviest food, was supposed to be eaten at the very end of meals.

◄ *Peasants picked apples from the orchard. They often baked their apples in pies or cooked them with nuts to make fruit puddings.*

Herbs and Spices in Medicine

Herbs and spices were used by wealthier people to make foods tastier and to cure headaches, **indigestion**, sore throats, and other ailments. As medications, herbs and spices were either mixed with food and drinks and swallowed, or mixed with ointment and applied to the skin. Some people made their own medicines, while others bought them from shops called apothecaries. Herbs and spices did not always cure illnesses, but they were the only medicine available to medieval people.

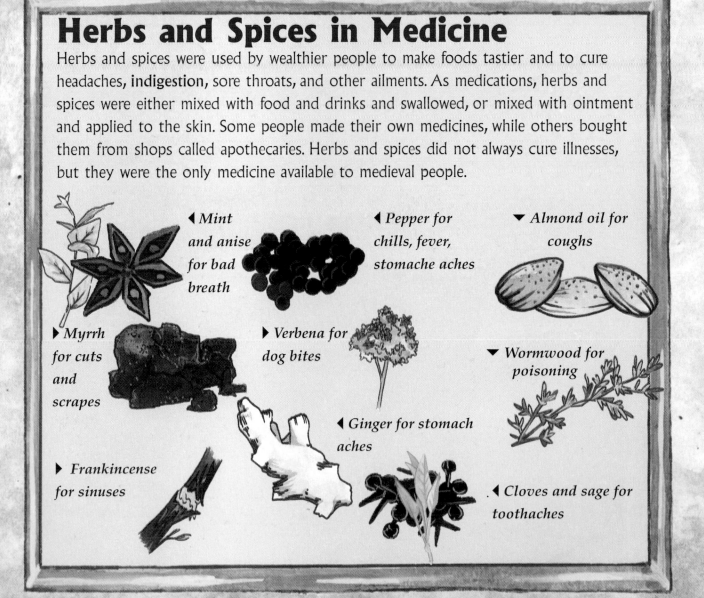

◄ *Mint and anise for bad breath*

◄ *Pepper for chills, fever, stomache aches*

▼ *Almond oil for coughs*

▶ *Myrrh for cuts and scrapes*

▶ *Verbena for dog bites*

▼ *Wormwood for poisoning*

▶ *Frankincense for sinuses*

◄ *Ginger for stomach aches*

◄ *Cloves and sage for toothaches*

Farming

Peasants worked all year growing food for themselves, the lord, and their livestock. Men, women, and children spent sunrise to sunset plowing fields, planting seeds, pulling out weeds, and harvesting crops.

Planting and harvesting were often done twice a year. In the spring, peasants planted oats, barley, peas, and beans, which they **harvested** in the autumn. In the autumn, they planted wheat and rye, which they harvested in the spring.

Beginning in the 1100s, peasants used a three-field system to grow crops. Spring crops were planted in one field, autumn crops in a second field, and the third field was left fallow, or empty, so the soil could regain its **nutrients**. The next year, the peasants rotated the crops and left a different field fallow.

Raising Livestock

Peasants also raised farm animals, such as horses and oxen, to pull their plows. Animals such as chickens, geese, pigs, sheep, goats, and cows were raised for food and wool. During the winter when the grazing land was frozen, it was difficult to keep the animals fed, so some of them were slaughtered. Pigs were the first to be killed because they only produced meat. Cows, sheep, and chickens were kept alive because they produced other useful items, including milk, wool, and eggs.

◀ *Only one animal was needed to pull plows through the light, dry soil of southern Europe, but it took two to six animals to pull heavy plows through the thick, moist soil of northern Europe. Since peasants usually owned only one animal, they shared their animals with one another.*

Peasants' Tools

Medieval peasants did most of the fieldwork with small, handheld tools, such as seed baskets, sickles, **scythes**, hoes, spades, rakes, and flails. When peasants began to use larger tools, such as heavy plows and harrows, farming became much faster and easier, and peasants were able to grow more food.

▲ Peasants carried seeds to the field in seed baskets woven from straw.

▲ Sickles were used to cut wheat, leaving short stalks behind on which animals grazed.

▲ Peasants swung flails to beat and separate grain from its stalk.

▲ Harrows were dragged behind plow animals to break up clumps of soil and remove weeds before seeds were planted.

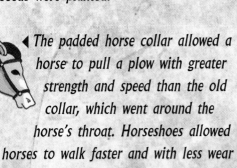

◄ The padded horse collar allowed a horse to pull a plow with greater strength and speed than the old collar, which went around the horse's throat. Horseshoes allowed horses to walk faster and with less wear and tear on their hoofs.

▲ Peasants in the drier regions of southern Europe moved water to and from fields using dams, drainage tunnels, canals, and water wheels that lifted water from rivers.

Peasants' Food

On strips of land in their fields and in small home gardens, peasants grew vegetables, such as cabbage, spinach, and onions, and herbs, such as garlic and parsley. They also grew apple, pear, and cherry trees, and they sometimes kept bees to make honey.

Peasant women cooked soups and stews in large pots, or cauldrons. The cauldrons were hung over open fires. A favorite stew was pottage, which was made of vegetables, herbs, bread crumbs, and sometimes bacon for extra flavor.

▸ *Peasants made ale by mixing barley and rye with herbs, honey, and water.*

▾ *Women or children fed the chickens and geese, cared for the chicks, and collected eggs for food.*

Bread and Ale

Two other important parts of the peasant's diet were a dark, brown bread made from barley and rye and a weak alcoholic drink called ale.

Peasants also ate eggs gathered from their chickens, and cheese and butter made from their cows' milk. Meat from chickens that no longer laid eggs, pork from pigs, fish from nearby ponds, and meat from cows were luxuries to many peasants, especially the very poor.

Preserving Food

Peasants who had meat and fish salted it to keep it from spoiling. With dry salting, they covered the food with salt for five to eight days. With brine curing, they soaked the food in brine, or salty water, for two to three days. In both cases, the salted meat and fish were hung on hooks to dry and then stored in barrels in a cool place. The food lasted up to three months without spoiling.

Vegetables, herbs, and fruits were also preserved. Vegetables were kept in jars of brine, vinegar, or mustard, and fruit and herbs were dried in the hot sun.

Cheese Wafers

Cheese wafers were served as a dessert on holidays and other special occasions. To make cheese wafers, beat four to six eggs in a bowl, then add a pinch of salt and enough flour to make a moist dough once everything is mixed together. Roll the dough into thin sheets and cut it into bite-size pieces. Cook the wafers in a frying pan coated with oil until they are golden brown on both sides. Put a piece of cheese between two wafers and heat in the frying pan until the cheese is melted.

▼ Peasants ate on benches at trestle tables. Trestle tables were made of boards placed on x-shaped supports, and could be easily taken apart. Most food was eaten with the fingers, except for soup, which was eaten with a spoon, and meat, which was cut with a knife.

Markets and Fairs

Peasants who had surplus, or extra, food gathered at popular meeting places, such as monasteries, churches, town squares, castles, city gates, and bridges. There, they sold their eggs, vegetables, herbs, fruit, cheeses, and homemade ale to people passing by.

Eventually, weekly markets were held at the meeting places. In addition to food, peasants sold livestock to butchers and other farmers. Townspeople set up stalls where they sold freshly baked bread, fresh meat, spices, pastries, and pies, as well as other goods, such as tools and clothes.

▲ *At village and town markets, food sellers displayed their goods on tables, on carts, in stalls, and in shop windows. Peddlers wandered around the marketplace selling goods from handheld baskets.*

Merchants from All Over

A much larger type of market was called a fair. Fairs took place once a year and lasted for days or even weeks. The most popular fairs in medieval Europe were in a region of northeastern France called Champagne, but other fairs took place in Germany, **Flanders**, Russia, and Switzerland. These fairs attracted **merchants** from all over Europe who traded cloth, dyes, jewelry, food, grain, and spices.

Some merchants sold more exotic foods from the **Middle East** and Asia, such as oranges, apricots, pomegranates, figs, and sugar. These items were rare and expensive and were a special treat for most fair visitors.

▲ *Grain merchants sold their product in sacks, but grain was measured by the bushel, half bushel, and quarter bushel, called a peck.*

Having Fun

Fairs were not only centers of trading, but also centers of entertainment. Dancers, musicians, jugglers, acrobats, and storytellers amused shoppers. Actors and puppeteers performed plays, while bears and monkeys did tricks. Local bakers, cooks, brewers, and winemakers prepared food and drink for fair visitors.

The Spice Trade

Merchants who traveled to faraway places, spice grocers, and apothecaries, who were like modern-day pharmacists, sold spices at fairs. The spices were so expensive that people locked them in cabinets and boxes so that they would not be stolen.

Spices improved the flavor of food. The spices saffron, cumin, and cloves were added to stewed beef, pork pies, and stuffed chicken. Desserts such as gingerbread and oat cakes could not be made without ginger and cinnamon. The spice called cardamom was mixed with wine to make spiced wine, and nutmeg and pepper were used to brew ale. Spices were also used in perfumes, cosmetics, medicines, and dyes.

Merchants from China, India, the Spice Islands, now called Indonesia, and the Middle East carried spices on ships that sailed from China to present-day Iraq. From there, **Arab** merchants transported the spices across the desert to ports on the Mediterranean Sea. Merchants from Italy picked up the spices and traveled back to Italian ports, especially those in Venice and Genoa.

▼ Once spices arrived in Italy, they were loaded onto boats and transported to cities and towns across Europe.

Wild Stories

To make sure European merchants did not take control of their part of the Spice Route, Arab merchants made up wild stories about how difficult it was to get spices. They said that men had to climb to the tops of mountains and snatch cinnamon sticks from large ferocious birds that lived in "cinnamon stick nests." Other valuable spices, they said, were protected by huge snakes and flesh-eating bats.

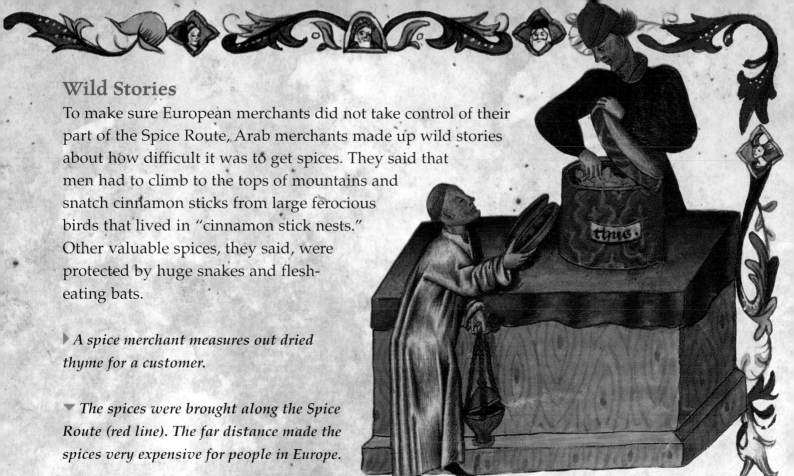

▶ *A spice merchant measures out dried thyme for a customer.*

▼ *The spices were brought along the Spice Route (red line). The far distance made the spices very expensive for people in Europe.*

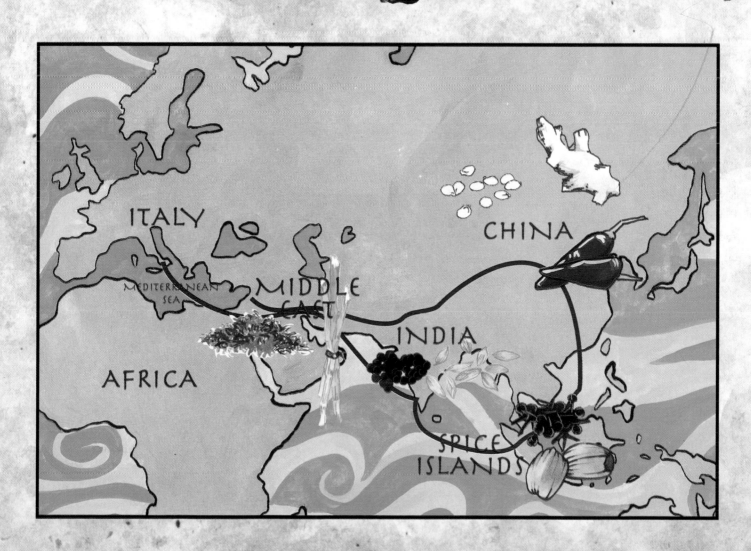

Eating in Towns

Townspeople had more choices of food than peasants because they lived close to markets and shops, but what they ate still depended on what they could afford. Craftspeople and their assistants grew vegetables and herbs in small home gardens to make soups and stews. They also raised cows, chickens, and pigs in pens behind their homes so they had cheese, butter, eggs, and bacon.

Wealthier merchants and master, or expert, craftspeople ate rabbit, pork, chicken, and beef that were flavored with spices. On special occasions, they enjoyed more expensive and rare meats, such as **venison**, lamb, and swan. They also ate many types of fish, cheese, fruit, bread, and other baked goods that they bought from shops in town. Ale or wine was served with every meal.

▼ *Inspectors visited tavern keepers and wine sellers each morning to sample their ale and wine. These inspectors, called wine criers, then went out into the streets to tell passersby about the wine and to offer samples. They also made sure the price of the ale and wine was fair.*

Preparing Food

Townswomen cooked soups and stews, fried eggs, bacon, and wafers, and roasted meats in open fires or in fireplaces. Meals were served in the main room of the house. Diners sat on benches and ate at trestle tables covered with tablecloths, which they used as napkins. The food was served on **pewter** plates or trenchers, which were plates made of wood or thick slices of stale bread. Bread trenchers soaked up juices from meat. They were eaten at the end of the meal or given to the poor or to the family dog.

Fire Safety

Fires always burned in medieval homes for cooking and warmth. If one house accidentally caught fire, other houses were soon up in flames and entire neighborhoods were destroyed. For safety, some towns required households to cover fires at night with large, round clay disks with **ventilation** holes. These covers were called couvres-feu, a French word that means "fire cover." A special bell, called a curfew, was rung in the evening to announce when to cover all fires.

Food Shops

On the ground floor of many town homes were shops that sold fresh meat, fish, poultry, cheese, bread, and pastries. Cookshops sold prepared foods, such as roasted meats, mincemeat pies, stewed chicken, puddings, and tarts filled with soft cheeses or eggs.

Butchers sold mutton, pork, beef, and lamb.

Cheesemongers bought cheese, butter, and other dairy products from peasants in the countryside and sold them to townspeople.

Fishmongers sold fish, such as cod, herring, turbot, and bass, as well as shellfish, such as oysters and mussels.

Poulterers sold slaughtered and live chickens, geese, and ducks.

Bakers baked wastel, an expensive bread made from fine white flour, for wealthier customers. They baked brown bread, made from less expensive bran and rye, for everyone else.

Tempting Customers

Like most medieval shops, shops that sold food usually had large windows that opened onto the street. The windows were covered by large shutters that folded down into shelves over the sidewalk. Food placed on the shelves tempted anyone who walked by.

In smaller towns, a variety of food shops were clustered together to make shopping easier. In larger towns, shops were often grouped together according to what they sold. Streets were sometimes named for their produce. London, England still has streets named Milk Street and Bread Street, where milk and bread were sold in the Middle Ages.

▼ *Colorful signs hung above shops to advertise their goods. In the Middle Ages, signs did not have words since many people could not read. Instead, there were pictures that everyone recognized.*

▼ *Taverns and inns were popular in the later Middle Ages. Taverns sold food and drink, while inns provided places to sleep as well.*

Cooking in the Castle

Castles housed nobles and their families, as well as knights, squires, **servants, guards, and castle officials. Large amounts of food were needed to feed everyone.**

In the Kitchen

Food for castle residents was prepared in large kitchens. Some kitchens were right inside castles and others were in separate buildings so that whole castles did not burn down if fires broke out. Some households cooked outdoors over roasting pits, where fires burned safely away from buildings.

Castle kitchens were very busy places. Several cooks worked under the careful eye of a master cook. Sauce cooks watched over soups, sauces, and boiled meats that cooked in cauldrons. The cauldrons hung by their handles from racks above the fire. The racks could be raised and lowered to control the cooking temperature. Soups and sauces were also cooked in smaller pots and in pans that stood on **trivets** above the fire.

▲ *Cooks carved meat, then placed it on plates that servers took to the nobles.*

▼ *Kitchen assistants, called turnspits, roasted pork, chicken, beef, and mutton on iron spits over open fires.*

Worktables

The kitchens were cluttered with long worktables, where assistants chopped vegetables, plucked poultry, cut fish, and carved meat. They used mortars and pestles, which were stone bowls and small stone clubs, to grind herbs and spices into powder. They also used graters to shave cheese, cloths to strain jellies, and stirring spoons to blend sauces. It was a scullion's job to clean up all the mess.

The Bakehouse

Bread was baked in a separate building called a bakehouse. The bakehouse had a dome-shaped oven heated by wood. Ovens were also used to bake pastries, such as honey cakes, fig pies, and cheese buns.

▼ *Bakers and their assistants used long wooden paddles to place and remove loaves of bread into and out of the oven.*

Storerooms

Near the kitchen were rooms where food and drinks were stored. The buttery held barrels of wine and ale, oils and vinegars, and empty containers in which liquids could be kept. The buttery got its name from the medieval French word *botte*, meaning "cask" or "barrel." Castles also had pantries, where breads and pies recently brought from the bakehouse were stored, along with cheese, butter, fruits, and spices.

▶ *Wine kept in the buttery was made from grapes that were crushed by foot. Medieval people usually mixed their wine with water to lessen the alcohol in the wine and to make it last longer.*

A Noble's Table

Nobles ate their meals in a private dining room or in the castle's main room, called the Great Hall. The Great Hall also served as a living room, meeting room, and sometimes even a bedroom.

Nobles usually dined with family members, guests, knights living in the castle, and castle officials. The lord, lady, and their most important guests sat at the high table, a table raised on a platform at one end of the Great Hall. An open container filled with salt, called a salt cellar, was placed in front of the most honored guest. The rest of the diners sat on benches at long, lower tables, called sideboards, which were said to be "below the salt."

Food was served to the high table first and then to the lower tables. The servers, called pages, were boys from other noble families who were sent to the noble's household to learn how to behave like knights and lords.

▲ *The lord and lady sat on comfortable chairs that were sometimes covered with a canopy to show how important the nobles were.*

Mealtime

In the Middle Ages, nobles ate three or four meals a day. Breakfast consisted of a small bit of bread and ale. The main meal, served between ten o'clock in the morning and noon, began with bread and soup. A meat dish, such as stewed beef with mustard, roasted pork stuffed with chestnuts, or lamb chops, followed. The next course was dessert, which usually consisted of cheeses or small cakes made with almonds, honey, or sugar. Wine accompanied the meal. An early supper, served between five and seven o'clock, consisted of a main dish, such as stewed chicken, served with bread and cheese.

▶ *If nobles were hungry before bedtime or if they were feeling sick, their servants brought them soup as a late-night snack.*

Table Manners

Proper manners were very important in the noble's dining hall. People in the Middle Ages ate mainly with their fingers, so they were expected to wash their hands before the meal and keep their hands clean during the meal by not picking their teeth, nails, or noses. Diners shared wine goblets, so it was considered polite for diners to wipe the grease from their mouths before putting their lips on the cups. People were supposed to eat slowly and take small bites. Soup was not to be slurped. Lastly, it was impolite to belch or pass gas at the table, to talk with one's mouth full, and to lean over the table.

▶ *Pages brought metal ewers filled with water to the tables so that diners could wash their hands before eating.*

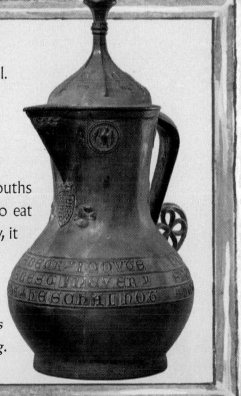

A Noble's Feast

On special occasions, such as the visit of a very important person, enormous feasts were held at the castle. Fruit, soups, and stews were followed by dishes of lamb, pork, fish, chicken, duck, or quail. Then, elaborate dishes such as whole roasted boars with apples in their mouths were brought into the Great Hall. There was also plenty of wine and sweets.

The butler and his assistants served wine and ale.

Pantlers delivered bread and butter to the table.

Carvers cut the meat or held the meat for the lord to carve with a long knife.

The steward oversaw the serving staff.

The hornblower announced that it was time to wash one's hands and begin the meal.

Linen tablecloths, glass or pewter goblets, trenchers, and wooden bowls covered the tables.

Cupbearers presented the lord's wine cup on bended knee.

Musicians and jugglers performed during and after the meal.

Hunting, Hawking, and Fishing

Nobles' tables were covered with a great variety of fresh meat, fowl, and fish. Nobles caught a lot of the meat and fowl themselves, by hunting.

Not only did hunting provide nobles with food, but it was also a social activity and a good way to get exercise. Hunting also prepared young noblemen for battle by teaching them horseback riding and **archery** skills.

Nobles went hunting in large groups called hunting parties. They caught large animals, such as deer and wild boars, using bows and arrows, or they sent hunting dogs to chase down and surround the animals. Then, the animals were killed with the thrust of a hunter's sword.

◀ Hunting parties included the lord, his hunting guests, horn blowers, who announced the beginning and end of the hunt, dogs that chased down the prey, and servants, called berners and fewterers, who handled the hounds.

Hunting with Birds

Nobles hunted small **prey** using a method of hunting called hawking. Hawks captured birds that flew higher than a bow and arrow could reach. They also swooped down to capture rabbits and squirrels from the ground. Then, the hawks delivered the prey to their masters.

Some people used another kind of bird, called a falcon, to hunt. This type of hunting was called falconry. It was expensive to hire someone to train hawks and falcons, the birds' training took a long time, and they needed to be cared for, housed, and fed, so only the wealthiest nobles hunted this way.

▲ *A large leather glove protected a hunter's hand from the sharp claws of a hawk or falcon.*

Fishing

The lord's manor usually had a fishpond stocked with trout, pike, or bass. Fish also swam in nearby rivers or the sea. Servants or fishers caught fish for the nobles using nets and baskets. They also used rods made of wood, fishing line made of hair from a horse's tail, wire hooks, and worms as bait.

▶ *Servants pulled in nets full of fish for the nobles.*

Feasts and Fasts

People in the Middle Ages celebrated many different feast days with large meals and festivals. Some feast days were religious holy days, such as Christmas, Easter, or a saint's day. Others were non-religious events, such as the end of the harvest.

Christmas

During the Christmas season, peasants were invited to dinner in the noble's Great Hall. The most important peasants, or those who farmed the most land, were treated to a meal of beef and bacon, chicken stew, good bread, and as much ale as they could drink. Less important peasants had to bring their own trenchers, cups, and napkins, and they were given bread, soup, ale, and a choice of different kinds of meat, such as beef, chicken, or mutton.

A popular game, called Bean King, was played at the dinner table. The baker baked loaves of bread with a bean hidden inside one loaf. Whichever guest received the slice with the bean in it became the Bean King and was the feast's honored guest.

Nobles' Christmas Feasts

At the Christmas feasts the nobles threw for their households, beautiful linens and candles covered the tables, and green foliage, such as holly, ivy, and mistletoe, decorated the walls. A large tree trunk, called a Yule, or Christmas, log burned in the fireplace.

Great amounts of fine spiced wine and food, including peacocks, swans, and the Yule boar, a full boar with an apple in its mouth, were served. Desserts included gingerbread, sweet plum pudding, and kings' cakes, which were sweet cakes made in the shape of a crown to symbolize the three kings who brought gifts to the baby Jesus.

▲ *Nobles were not at the same Christmas feasts as the peasants. Instead, they entertained their knights, ladies-in-waiting, and castle officials at a much more elaborate banquet.*

Feast Days

Special foods were served on certain feast days. St. Martin's Day, celebrated on November 11 to honor Saint Martin, was also known as the Feast of the Plowman. On this day, the lord and lady of the manor hosted a dinner for peasants who worked in their fields. The dinner featured foods made with grain that the plowmen grew, including loaves of bread, ale, oat cakes, and frumenty, which was wheat boiled in milk and seasoned with cinnamon and sugar.

▲ *During and after feasts, **minstrels**, jugglers, and musicians entertained guests. Mummers, who were actors dressed up in fanciful costumes, also put on plays and danced for their audiences.*

Fast Days

Unlike on feast days, on fast days people were only allowed to eat a little bit of food, usually one small meal at noon, and they could not eat meat. Instead, they ate fish, eggs, or vegetables. Fridays, the night before important holy days, and the 40-day period before Easter, called Lent, were fast days according to the Church. For the most religious people, Wednesdays and Saturdays were also fast days.

▼ *For weeks after a successful harvest, food was plentiful and peasants enjoyed feasts with one another.*

Food in Other Cultures

I n the Middle Ages, people around the world had different diets depending on the crops that grew where they lived. Many of their foods were introduced to Europe after the Middle Ages, including potatoes and tomatoes, which were first eaten in North, Central, and South America.

South America

In South America, the Incas built fields on steep mountain slopes where they grew potatoes and a grain called quinoa, which they ground into flour. The lower valleys were better suited for growing **maize**, beans, chili peppers, tomatoes, potatoes, and squash. Scattered throughout the valleys were cherry, peach, and plum orchards. The Incas also hunted llamas, deer, and guinea pigs for their meat. *Chicha*, an alcoholic drink made from corn, potatoes, peanuts, or grain, was a popular Inca beverage.

▲ *Incas lived in the mountains, so the only place they could grow food was on terraced hillsides. The terraces kept water from running down the sides of the mountains and eroding the soil.*

West Africa

The people of West Africa grew two types of grains called millet and sorghum. They used these grains to make bread, an alcoholic drink called beer, and a thick, soft porridge. They also grew peas, peppers, nuts, and rice. They raised chickens for eggs, and kept cows, camels, and goats for milk and meat. West Africans did not eat much pork since many were **Muslim**, and their religion, Islam, forbade it.

◀ *The people of West Africa used millet to feed themselves and their livestock.*

▲ *Chinampas were made by piling up soil from the bottom of lakes to form "floating gardens" on which crops were grown.*

Central America

Aztec farmers in Tenochtitlan, now Mexico City, grew squash, beans, chili peppers, and maize in *chinampas*, which were gardens built on lakes. Aztec women used the maize to make bread and flat cakes called tortillas. Aztec men hunted turkeys, pheasants, ducks, venison, wild boar, and rabbits for their meat. Chocolate, made from ground cocoa beans mixed with water and sometimes honey or vanilla, was a favorite drink of Aztec nobles.

India

People from the hot, southern parts of India grew rice, which they ground into flour and used to make a moist bread. People in the cooler north grew wheat and barley, which they used to make a dry, flat bread. Medieval India's main foods also included beans, peas, chickpeas, nuts, and fresh fruit, such as mangoes and coconuts. Foods were seasoned with pepper, cardamom, and other spices. Farmers kept chickens for their eggs and meat, and goats and dairy cattle for their milk. People's diets also depended on their religion. India's **Hindus** did not eat beef, and its Muslims did not eat pork.

▼ *Indian farmers planted rice in small fields divided by dirt walls that held water inside. The farmers drained the water when it was time to harvest the rice.*

31

Glossary

Arab A person from the Middle East or North Africa who speaks the Arabic language

archery The sport of shooting with a bow and arrow

Christmas A Christian holiday celebrating the birth of Jesus Christ

digest To break down food in the stomach into substances that the body can use

Easter A Christian holiday celebrating Jesus Christ's return to life after he was killed

erode To wear away gradually, as with wind and rain wearing away mountain peaks

Flanders A Dutch-speaking region of northern Belgium

harvest The gathering of crops

Hindu A person who follows the ancient Indian religion of Hinduism. Hindus worship one creator power, Brahman, and many gods and goddesses, whom they consider different forms of Brahman

indigestion Pain caused when the body has difficulty digesting food

knight A medieval soldier who fought on horseback, mainly with swords

livestock Farm animals

maize Corn

merchant A person who buys and sells goods

Middle East A region that is made up of southwestern Asia and northern Africa

minstrel A person who entertains by singing or reciting poetry

monastery A building where religious men called monks live and work

Muslim A person who believes in Islam, a religion based on the teachings of Allah and his prophets

mutton Sheep meat

nutrient A substance that living things need in order to grow

pewter A metal made of tin with a little lead, used to make dishes and utensils

prey An animal hunted by another animal for food

saint's day A day that honors a Christian holy person, called a saint

scythe A tool with a long, curved blade and long handle, used to cut crops

squire A young nobleman training to be a knight

trivet A three-legged stand made of metal, used for supporting cooking vessels in a hearth

venison Deer meat

ventilation The movement of fresh air

Index

1 2 3 4 5 6 7 8 9 0   Printed in the U.S.A.   0 9 8 7 6 5 4